DO MATH WITH SPORTS STATS!

NASCAR

Stats, Facts,

BY KATE MIKOLEY

Gareth Stevens
PUBLISHING

Please visit our website, www.garethstevens.com. For a free color catalog of all our high-quality books, call toll free 1-800-542-2595 or fax 1-877-542-2596.

Cataloging-in-Publication Data

Names: Mikoley, Kate.
Title: NASCAR: stats, facts, and figures / Kate Mikoley.
Description: New York : Gareth Stevens Publishing, 2018. | Series: Do math with sports stats! | Includes index.
Identifiers: LCCN ISBN 9781538211410 (pbk.) | ISBN 9781538211434 (library bound) | ISBN 9781538211427 (6 pack)
Subjects: LCSH: NASCAR (Association)–Juvenile literature. | Stock car racing–Mathematics–Juvenile literature.
Classification: LCC GV1029.9.S74 M47 2018 | DDC 796.720151–dc23

First Edition

Published in 2018 by
Gareth Stevens Publishing
111 East 14th Street, Suite 349
New York, NY 10003

Copyright © 2018 Gareth Stevens Publishing

Designer: Samantha DeMartin
Editor: Kate Mikoley

Photo credits: pp. 4–29 (paperclips) AVS-Images/Shutterstock.com; covers, pp. 1–29 (pencil) irin-k/Shutterstock.com; pp. 4–29 (post-its) Pixel Embargo/Shutterstock.com; pp. 4–29 (tape) Flas100/Shutterstock.com; pp. 3–32 (graph paper) BLACKDAY/Shutterstock.com; covers, pp. 1–32 (bleacher texture) Al Sermeno Photography/Shutterstock.com; covers, pp. 1–29 (clipboard) Mega Pixel/Shutterstock.com; covers, pp. 1–29 (formula overlay) lolya1988/Shutterstock.com; covers, pp. 1–29 (index card) photastic/Shutterstock.com; cover, p. 1 Chris Graythen/Getty Images Sport/Getty Images; pp. 5, 8, 13 (top), 19, 25, 27 (both) Action Sports Photography/Shutterstock.com; pp. 6, 7, 9 RacingOne/ISC Archives/Getty Images; pp. 10, 29 Daniel Hurlimann/Shutterstock.com; p. 11 Jerry Markland/Getty Images Sport/Getty Images; p. 13 (background) EPG_EuroPhotoGraphics/Shutterstock.com; p. 14 Kevin Norris/Shutterstock.com; p. 15 Sean Gardner/Getty Images Sport/Getty Images; p. 16 Sarah Crabill/NASCAR/Getty Images; p. 17 Jared C. Tilton/Getty Images Sport/Getty Images; p. 18 Elsa/Getty Images Sport/Getty Images; p. 21 (background) Fabio Pagani/Shutterstock.com; p. 21 (photo) Icon Sports Wire/Icon Sportswire/Getty Images; pp. 22 (D-shaped oval), 23 (quad-oval) Odysseus1479/Wikimedia Commons; p. 22 (tri-oval) Will Pittenger/Wikimedia Commons; p. 23 (oval) Nascar1996/Wikimedia Commons; p. 23 (triangle) Pitlane02/Wikimedia Commons; p. 23 (photo) Jonathan Ferrey/NASCAR/Getty Images; p. 24 Doug Pensinger/Getty Images Sport/Getty Images.

Printed in the United States of America

CPSIA compliance information: Batch #CW18GS: For further information contact Gareth Stevens, New York, New York at 1-800-542-2595.

CONTENTS

Let's Race! 4

Racing in Daytona 8

The Premier Series 10

Learn the Points 12

Lots of Laps 16

Start Your Engines 18

What's Your Average? 20

Stay on Track 22

Flying the Flags 24

Slowing Down 26

A Team Sport 28

Glossary 30

For More Information 31

Index 32

Words in the glossary appear in **bold** type the first time they are used in the text.

LET'S RACE!

Dozens of cars dart around the track. Thousands of fans pack the stands to cheer on their favorite drivers. Millions more watch from home. With each **lap** around the track, the excitement grows. Which car will be the first to cross the finish line? Will it be the crowd favorite, or will it be the **underdog**?

"NASCAR" stands for the National Association for Stock Car Auto Racing.

RACING STATS

NASCAR is more than a bunch of cars driving around a track. Numbers and math play a big part in these popular events. Statistics, or stats, are numbers that represent information. Stats show how well someone is doing at a certain skill. Some stats are easy to follow, but others take a bit more thinking to figure out!

Originally, stock cars were just regular cars that people also raced in. Today, the automobiles we call stock cars are built specially to be raced. Because it's the main governing body of stock car racing, many simply call the sport NASCAR.

EVERY NASCAR RACE IS A LITTLE DIFFERENT. MANY RACES LAST FOR MORE THAN 400 MILES (644 KM). DRIVERS OFTEN COMPLETE HUNDREDS OF LAPS AROUND THE TRACK!

Stock car racing got its start in the early 1900s. By the late 1930s, these events had become very popular, but they were often not very well organized. Rules were different depending on the track, and some tracks didn't have a safe amount of room for all the people who attended. By the late 1940s, that all changed.

THE NUMBERS GAME

NASCAR IS ALL ABOUT THE SPEED! TODAY, CARS USED IN NASCAR ARE SOMETIMES ABLE TO REACH SPEEDS HIGHER THAN 200 MILES PER HOUR! IF A CAR IS **CONSISTENTLY** GOING 150 MILES PER HOUR FOR 4 HOURS, HOW MANY MILES HAS THE CAR DRIVEN? ANSWER ON PAGE 29.

NASCAR began after a group of racetrack owners and drivers met in Daytona Beach, Florida, in 1947. A man named Bill France, who was already involved in the racing world, organized the meeting. He's often considered the force behind establishing the organization. The first official NASCAR race happened in 1948.

BEFORE NASCAR WAS FORMED, BILL FRANCE HAD ALREADY ORGANIZED MANY RACING EVENTS, INCLUDING A YEARLONG SERIES OF RACES CALLED THE NATIONAL CHAMPIONSHIP STOCK CAR CIRCUIT.

RACING IN DAYTONA

Before NASCAR, Daytona Beach was already a popular spot for stock car racing. After the group was formed, Daytona Beach became its official headquarters. Today, it's home to the Daytona International Speedway and one of the most popular races in NASCAR.

The Daytona 500 was first held in 1959. This first race was attended by 41,000 fans. Since then, the 500-mile (805 km) race has been held every February. Today, more than 100,000 fans pack the stands. The track is 2.5 miles (4 km) long, so drivers must take 200 laps around the track. The race often lasts for more than 3 hours!

THE NUMBERS GAME

IN NASCAR, DRIVERS OFTEN MAKE PIT STOPS. DURING THESE STOPS, A CREW MIGHT HELP MAKE REPAIRS AND FILL THE CAR WITH GAS. IF A DRIVER IN THE DAYTONA 500 MAKES A PIT STOP AFTER COMPLETING 1/8 OF THE RACE, HOW MANY LAPS HAVE THEY ALREADY DRIVEN? ANSWER ON PAGE 29.

$$200 \times \frac{1}{8}$$

Lee and Richard Petty

DARLINGTON INTERNATIONAL RACEWAY

HERE ON MAY 13, 1967, RICHARD PETTY SET AN ALL-TIME NASCAR RECORD BY STREAKING TO VICTORY IN THE REBEL 400, IN A 1967 PLYMOUTH. IT WAS HIS 55TH CAREER GRAND NATIONAL WIN, TOPPING THE PREVIOUS CAREER HIGH OF 54, SET BY HIS FATHER, LEE PETTY.

SEPT. 4, 1967

LEE PETTY WON THE FIRST DAYTONA 500 IN 1959. HIS SON, RICHARD, WENT ON TO WIN THE EVENT SEVEN TIMES!

THE PREMIER SERIES

The NASCAR season consists of many races and series. The premier series, or main group of races, in the sport has had many different names over the years. It was originally called the Strictly Stock Series, but was soon renamed the Grand National Series. After a few more name changes, it became the Monster Energy NASCAR Cup Series in 2017.

IN 2016, JIMMIE JOHNSON WON HIS SEVENTH NASCAR CUP SERIES, TYING WITH RICHARD PETTY AND DALE EARNHARDT FOR MOST CUP SERIES TITLES.

A points system is used to decide a champion within a series of races. The driver with the most points at the end of the series is the champion! Like the names of the events, the points systems have changed many times over the years.

Driver Danica Patrick before a Cup Series race

THE NUMBERS GAME

THE PREMIER SERIES OF NASCAR IS OFTEN JUST REFERRED TO AS THE "CUP SERIES." THERE ARE 36 RACES IN THE CUP SERIES.

IF A CAR IS 36 INCHES FROM THE FINISH LINE, HOW MANY FEET AWAY IS IT? REMEMBER, THERE ARE 12 INCHES IN 1 FOOT. ANSWER ON PAGE 29.

LEARN THE POINTS

Before 2016, up to 43 cars could race in each NASCAR Cup Series event. In 2016, NASCAR changed the rules so that the **maximum** number of cars that can race in each Cup Series event became 40.

The points system is set up so that the driver who finishes in first place gets 40 points. The driver who finishes the race in second place gets 35 points. Each finisher after that scores one fewer point than the finisher before them. This continues all the way down to the 36th finisher. The 36th through 40th finishers all get 1 point each.

THE NUMBERS GAME

THERE'S A SIMPLE WAY TO **CALCULATE** HOW MANY POINTS A DRIVER WHO CAME BETWEEN SECOND AND 36TH PLACE GETS. FIRST, TAKE THE NUMBER OF THE PLACE THEY CAME IN AND ADD 3. THEN, SUBTRACT THAT ANSWER FROM 40. IF A DRIVER CAME IN 23RD PLACE, HOW MANY POINTS DO THEY GET? ANSWER ON PAGE 29.

$$40 - (23 + 3)$$

HAS CHANGED MANY TIMES. AT ONE TIME, THE POINTS HAD TO DO WITH HOW MUCH MONEY A RACE PAID! IT WASN'T UNTIL THE 1970S THAT A SYSTEM SIMILAR TO THE ONE USED TODAY WAS PUT IN PLACE.

In 2017, NASCAR added a new way to score points in series races. Each race includes three "stages" or parts. In addition to the points earned after the final stage, or end of the race, drivers can earn extra points by being in the top 10 at the end of stage 1 or stage 2.

Sometimes, a driver may need to stop driving after the race has started. When this happens, another driver, called a relief driver, can take over. Relief drivers don't earn points. The driver who started the race is the one who receives the points.

OTHER SERIES IN NASCAR ALSO USE THE STAGE FORMAT. IN THE TRUCK SERIES, SHOWN HERE, DRIVERS RACE PICKUP TRUCKS!

THE NUMBERS GAME

THE NUMBER OF LAPS IN EACH STAGE DEPENDS ON THE RACE. LET'S SAY A RACE HAS A TOTAL OF 325 LAPS. IF THE FIRST TWO STAGES ARE EACH 85 LAPS, HOW MANY LAPS ARE THERE IN THE FINAL STAGE OF THE RACE? ANSWER ON PAGE 29.

$$325 - (85 \times 2)$$

LOTS OF LAPS

Laps are an important part of NASCAR. Some races have hundreds of laps, but each lap is important. During a race, the lead lap is the lap that the leader is currently on. If the leader has completed at least one full lap more than other cars, those other cars are considered "lapped traffic."

Some drivers complete more than 10,000 laps in a series each season! A driver's laps completed percentage takes into account the laps a driver didn't finish. A stat called laps led keeps track of how many laps the driver was in the lead for.

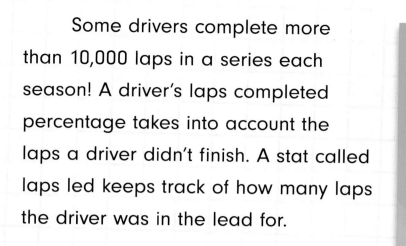

A CLOSE FINISH IS SOMETIMES CALLED A PHOTO FINISH. BEFORE ELECTRONIC TIMING, JUDGES HAD TO LOOK AT PHOTOS OF THE FINISH TO DECIDE WHO WON A CLOSE RACE!

START YOUR ENGINES

Every fraction of a second in a NASCAR race is important. Even the moments that happen before the race starts can make a difference. A driver's starting position can help them begin the race ahead of the **competition**.

A driver's starting position is usually decided by how well they do in the qualifying process. Different races and series sometimes have different qualifying rules, but most of the time, the better a driver does in the qualifying run, the better starting position they will get. The fastest qualifier gets the pole position, or the top starting position.

IN A QUALIFYING RUN, DRIVERS GO ONE AT A TIME. THEY GET 2 LAPS OF THE TRACK, AND THE FASTEST LAP IS THEIR QUALIFYING TIME.

NASCAR races are fast, but they're also long. There's plenty of time for other cars to catch up, so a good starting position doesn't always mean a driver will win the race. In 2000, Jeff Gordon started a race at the Talladega Superspeedway in the 36th position and ended up winning!

WHAT'S YOUR AVERAGE?

One way to judge a driver's abilities is by looking at their averages. An average start shows the average starting position that a driver begins their races in. For example, a driver who has started every race with the pole position would have a starting average of 1. This is extremely rare, but could happen if a driver's only been in a couple of races.

A driver's average finish shows the average position where they finished their races. For example, if a driver had won every race they'd been in, they would have an average finish of 1.

THE NUMBERS GAME

TO FIND A DRIVER'S AVERAGE START, YOU ADD EACH OF THEIR STARTING POSITIONS TOGETHER AND DIVIDE THAT NUMBER BY THEIR TOTAL RACES. LET'S SAY A DRIVER WAS IN 4 RACES. IF SHE STARTED EACH OF THE 4 RACES IN 5TH POSITION, WHAT WAS HER AVERAGE START? ANSWER ON PAGE 29.

A DRIVER'S AVERAGES ARE A GOOD WAY TO GET AN IDEA OF THEIR POSITIONS, BUT ONE HIGH POSITION CAN SWAY THEIR AVERAGE, SO IT'S BEST TO LOOK AT ALL THEIR INDIVIDUAL POSITIONS.

STAY ON TRACK

Every NASCAR track is different. Some are almost 3 miles (4.8 km) all the way around, while others aren't even 1 mile (1.6 km)!

Most tracks are considered oval in shape, but in the NASCAR world, there are a few different kinds of ovals. A "true oval" track has two longer, flatter sides and two curved ends. A tri-oval is a mix between a true oval and a triangle, meaning it has an extra curve on one of the sides. There are also D-shaped oval and quad-oval tracks. Driving on an oval track involves turning in only one direction, usually to the left.

DAYTONA INTERNATIONAL
SPEEDWAY
TRI-OVAL

KANSAS SPEEDWAY
D-SHAPED OVAL

THE ROAD COURSE

There's one type of course in NASCAR that's very different from an oval track. This is the road course. Road courses include left and right turns. Some think road courses are more difficult than oval tracks because of all the twists and turns. Others think ovals are tougher because they're raced at faster speeds and can be more dangerous.

Watkins Glen International

THE POCONO RACEWAY IN PENNSYLVANIA IS MORE OF A TRIANGLE THAN MOST TRI-OVAL TRACKS. BECAUSE OF ITS THREE SHARP TURNS, PEOPLE HAVE NICKNAMED IT THE "TRICKY TRIANGLE."

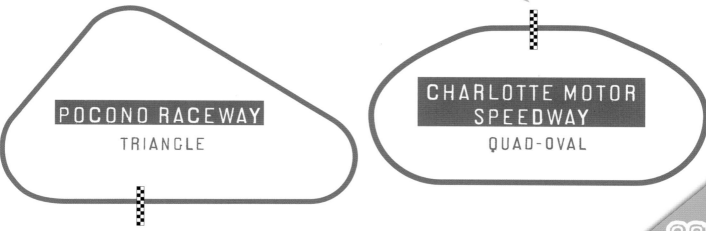

MARTINSVILLE SPEEDWAY
OVAL

POCONO RACEWAY
TRIANGLE

CHARLOTTE MOTOR SPEEDWAY
QUAD-OVAL

FLYING THE FLAGS

If you've ever watched a NASCAR race, you've probably seen a few different flags waving on the track. The most well-known flag in racing is the black-and-white checkered flag. This is waved when the winner crosses the finish line.

THE PERSON WHO WAVES THE FLAG IS CALLED THE FLAGMAN. FLAGMEN STAND IN AN AREA ABOVE THE FINISH LINE.

Other flags also help officials communicate messages to drivers. For example, green, red, and yellow flags have meanings similar to the colors on a traffic light. Green flags are shown at the start of the race. Yellow flags mean drivers should slow down and exercise **caution**, and red flags mean the race must stop.

THE NUMBERS GAME

CHECKERED FLAGS SOMETIMES LOOK SLIGHTLY DIFFERENT, BUT THEY'RE USUALLY RECTANGULAR IN SHAPE. IF A RECTANGULAR FLAG HAS A LENGTH OF 7 SQUARES AND A WIDTH OF 5 SQUARES, HOW MANY TOTAL SQUARES ARE ON THE FLAG? REMEMBER, YOU CAN FIND THE AREA OF A RECTANGLE BY MULTIPLYING ITS LENGTH BY ITS WIDTH. ANSWER ON PAGE 29.

SLOWING DOWN

NASCAR wouldn't be the sport it is if it weren't for its speedy cars, but the fast speeds can be dangerous. Wrecks or accidents are part of the sport, but safety is still important. That's why some big tracks require cars to have restrictor plates. These are thin pieces of metal that limit the amount of air that goes into the engine. This lowers the car's **horsepower** and speed.

Restrictor plates are meant to make NASCAR safer, but some people think they actually make it more dangerous. Since the cars can't drive as fast, they often race very close together. If one car crashes, others might also crash.

THE NUMBERS GAME

EVEN WITH RESTRICTOR PLATES, CARS REACH SPEEDS NEAR 200 MILES PER HOUR. RESTRICTOR PLATES ARE SAID TO REDUCE DRIVING SPEEDS BY ABOUT 10 MILES PER HOUR. IF THIS IS TRUE, HOW FAST COULD A CAR THAT GOES 187 MILES PER HOUR WITH RESTRICTOR PLATES GO WITHOUT THEM? CAN YOU ROUND THE ANSWER TO THE NEAREST 10? ANSWER ON PAGE 29.

RESTRICTOR PLATES ARE MOST OFTEN USED ON LARGER TRACKS, SUCH AS THE TALLADEGA SUPERSPEEDWAY AND DAYTONA INTERNATIONAL SPEEDWAY.

A TEAM SPORT

The crew is an important part of each NASCAR team. This is a group of people who make sure the car is in the best possible condition. Crews include a chief, or leader, and engineers. They also include people who are very skilled in working on specific parts of the car, such as engine specialists and tire specialists. The people who help make repairs and keep the car running on race day are called the pit crew.

THE PIT STOP

Every second a car sits at a pit stop is time that could be used to win the race. Pit crews need to work fast! A good crew can get the car in and out of the stop in 12 seconds! This includes changing all 4 tires, filling up the gas **tank**, and making small repairs.

It might seem like NASCAR is all about the drivers, but it's actually a team sport! There are many people who help get each car to the finish line.

ANSWER KEY

p. 6 – 600 miles

p. 9 – 25 laps

p. 11 – 3 feet

p. 12 – 14 points

p. 15 – 155 laps

p. 20 – 5

p. 25 – 35 squares

p. 26 – 197 miles per hour; rounded – 200 miles per hour

EACH PERSON ON THE PIT CREW HAS A JOB. FROM CARRYING THE TIRES TO FILLING THE TANK, EACH POSITION IS IMPORTANT.

GLOSSARY

accurate: free from mistakes

calculate: to figure something out using math

caution: care, thoughtfulness, and close attention to avoid risks

competition: the person or group you are competing with

consistently: always acting or behaving the same way

horsepower: the measure of the power produced by an engine

lap: an act of going completely around a track or over a course

maximum: the highest number or amount that is possible or allowed

tank: a large vessel for storing things, such as gas for a car

underdog: a person or team that is expected to lose a contest or race

FOR MORE INFORMATION

BOOKS

Mahaney, Ian F. *The Math of NASCAR*. New York, NY: PowerKids Press, 2012.

Young, Jeff C. *Dropping the Flag: Auto Racing*. Edina, MN: ABDO Publishing, 2011.

WEBSITES

NASCAR

www.nascar.com

Keep up with the latest stats and your favorite drivers on the official NASCAR site.

Quiz! NASCAR Trivia

www.kidzworld.com/quiz/4479-quiz-nascar-trivia

Test your knowledge of NASCAR trivia with this fun quiz.

Publisher's note to educators and parents: Our editors have carefully reviewed these websites to ensure that they are suitable for students. Many websites change frequently, however, and we cannot guarantee that a site's future contents will continue to meet our high standards of quality and educational value. Be advised that students should be closely supervised whenever they access the Internet.

2-19

INDEX

average finish 20

average starting position 20

crew 9, 28, 29

Cup Series 10, 11, 12

Daytona 500 8, 9

Daytona Beach 7, 8

Daytona International
        Speedway 8, 27

Earnhardt, Dale 10

flags 24, 25

France, Bill 7

Gordon, Jeff 19

Johnson, Jimmie 10

laps 4, 5, 8, 15, 16, 17, 18

laps completed
        percentage 17

laps led 17

Patrick, Danica 11

Petty, Richard 9, 10

Pocono Raceway 23

pit stops 9, 28

points 11, 12, 13, 14

pole position 18, 20

qualifying 18

restrictor plates 26, 27

stages 14, 15

starting position 18, 19, 20

Talladega Superspeedway
        19, 27

track 4, 5, 6, 8, 17, 18, 22, 23,
        24, 26, 27

truck series 15